Drama Of Life: Sonnets And Music

William Platt

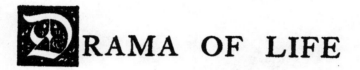

DRAMA OF LIFE

Sonnets and Music

By
WILLIAM PLATT

Author of " The Staff in Flower," " The Maid Lilias,"
" The Blossoming of Tansy," " London and Londoners,"
" Child Music," etc.

LONDON
EVAN YELLON
The Celtic Press
38 CHANCERY LANE, W.C.
1908

Drama of Life

Dedicated to
My Wife
and to
The Tayport Art Circle
(Stewart Carmichael, Alec. Grieve,
David Foggie, James Douglas;
and the Memory of
Charles Mills and Frank Laing)

See Sonnet 22.

Contents

MUSICAL PRELUDE
"Is Life Enough?"

(See Sonnet 48)

DRAMA OF LIFE

Consisting of 56 Sonnets divided into Six Sections
as follows :—

CONTENTS

MUSICAL POSTLUDE
"Life is Enough!"
(See Sonnet 51)

IS LIFE ENOUGH?

PRELUDE.

"IS LIFE ENOUGH?"

NOTE.—The Composer fully believes that the light and shade indicated in any given piece are only general directions, and that all expressive music demands something fuller than any possible markings of *f* and *p*.

The Orchestral score of this Prelude may be borrowed from the Composer.

Notes in brackets may be omitted with a view to simplification.

The Orchestral score of this Prelude may be borrowed from the Composer.

LIFE IN MASS

B

I

Drama of Life

PASSION and pathos, love, hate, grandeur, sin,
  Ev'ry extreme in ev'ry compound blent
  Dazzles the eyes of him who looks within
The heart of Man, and straightway is intent
To study all the wondrous gospel there.
  An endless study and a deep delight,
From 'neath convention's trappings to lay bare
  The soul, and feel its sanity and might.
Well might we live for this and nothing more;
  Just to discover Man in his estate;
With tense emotion thrilling to the core,
Meet for the highest or the humblest fate.

O human soul! Thee truly to have known
And truly loved, were better than a throne!

Life and Youth

THE youth in fancy meditates on life,
    As dreaming maidens meditate on love ;
        Not knowing what awaits in this tense strife
Of good and ill ; e'en as a new-fledged dove
Knows not the hawk, nor her own strength of wing ;
    Just as young wives know not the travail stern,
Nor yet the great rich joy the child will bring.
    In school as in a swimming-bath we learn ;
When we adventure on the raging Sea
    Time after time on our full length we're flung ;
Fierce is the struggle, happy still are we,
    Though the bent back with pebbly hail is stung.

O youth and maid, still shuddering on life's brink,
Life is more grand and desperate than ye think !

III

A Verdict

CALM lay the dead; his share of heat all spent;
    Just a mere wilful, ordinary man.
            His wife stood by, her grief more eloquent
Because no tear across her pale cheek ran.
The friends passed in, they had no word to give her;
    When hearts would speak, words are too seldom rife;
What could they say that could one pang relieve her?
    Just a mere loving, ordinary wife.
At last one came and gazed upon his friend,
    And looked again upon the woman there;
He knew their life, its modest scope and end;
    Just a mere struggling, ordinary pair.
He knew their faults, their strife, their love and bliss;
    He sighed; then said "How beautiful he is."

IV

Familiar Things

FAMILIAR things, how they increase in beauty !
    The rose, and woman's bosom never tire us ;
    Fantastic things pall on us. Simple duty,
The needful daily round, these still inspire us.
The wife of honeymoon is not so dear
    In her glad radiance as when she hath past
In loving wifehood many a blissful year,
    And each day swells the joyous store of the last.
The tender intimate things of life are dearest ;
    The flow'rs next our own doorstep we love best ;
Great men are greatest to their very nearest ;
    In homeliness is our true self expressed.

Call ye him Hero who one loud scene plays ?
What call ye him who's brave through life's dull days ?

V

Pollen

THE air is rich with perfume ; everywhere
  The flowerets' glow makes sweet the ways of
   life ;
The needful Mystery infects the air ;
 With warm fertility each breath is rife.
The pollen seeks the chalice ; the decree
 Of God rules o'er the hillside and the vale ;
Hark to the eager murmurings of the bee ;
 See how the stress makes the chaste lily pale.
Be glad, O Man, the harvest still is sure ;
 Nature is fertile, Nature loves increase ;
The pollen's miracle must still endure ;
 Time's self shall die before the seed shall cease.

Now is the moment ; at this very hour
The Mystery thrills deep each life-swept flower.

VI

The Generations

ERE, where the folk are all on holiday
   The roll of generations is well seen.
   Watch those bright youngsters merrily at play
With their grand-parents ; note the tender mien
Of mothers and of fathers with their young ;
   Then unto those rapt couples turn an eye
Who by love's burning darts are keenly stung
   To mating and increase. A century
Shall pass, and not one soul of these remain.
   Yea, but Love's harvest, ever reaped and sown,
Shall give us all our losses back again,
   Sap of our very sap, bone of our bone.

All in a bed of down Man's future lies ;
Love shall awake her, kissing her soft eyes.

VII

Abundance

THE elements of beauty and of force
  In life, so inexhaustible, so rich ;
  The infinite variety, resource ;
The never-ending bold surprises which
Sustain our drama and arouse our souls. . . .
  O, how can I express it ! While I gaze,
Amazement on amazement freshly rolls
  With dazzle and bewilderment ablaze !
I, like a stammering, overwhelmèd child
  Lost in the glamour of a million toys,
Know that life's store of wonder, mountain-piled,
  Beggars my words, makes silent my weak voice.

Joy, laughter, madness, work, crime, hate, love, tears,
Astounding life makes mock of our grey fears.

Acceptance

THOU deathless, boundless God, Thy pageant
world
    With tense, awe-smiting contrast is illumed ;
From dark to light with equal passion hurled ;
    Life warmed by fire, yet in that fire consumed.
The cornfield draws its strength from Earth and air,
    Eager as mother's milk, our needs to quench ;
But storm, drought, earthquake, lay Earth's bowels bare,
    The breast is milkless, our weak lips unclench.
Then Man himself, heir both to sky and dust,
    These strenuous extremes intensifies ;
Merciless, mad, the fury of his lust,
    Yet for his friend, his cause, he fights, he dies.

Thus is God's drama ; thus its matchless force.
We bow, we atoms sprinkled in His course.

LIFE IN ASPECTS

IX

Sin

THE best can not live sinless; and the worst
　　By many an act of goodness is redeemed.
　　Some secret sin each in himself hath cursed;
The lowest wretch in moments fair hath dreamed
Of a new Heaven and new earth unrolled
　　Before the eyes of hope and faith and him;
The dullest sky hath somewhere dawn's bright gold;
　　True is the utterance of the Cherubim :—
Holy the God Who made us; holy all;
　　Holy each birth and every lovers' tryst;
Holy the eternal moment of the fall,
　　Needing the ceaseless sacrifice, the Christ!

The grandeur of the struggle, lose or win,
Grows from our strong black adversary, Sin.

X

Work

AND we are stripped for labour . . . Good, O
good !
The brain alert, the muscles swinging free
Work is the cure for every sullen mood ;
  Joy is a door, and travail holds the key.
" I can achieve," a motto sweet and great :
  In sweat and toil and anguish, " I achieve."
" I can achieve," then I have mastered fate ;
  To do is still the best way to believe.
Work thou art good ; work in whatever form,
  Blacksmith or goldsmith, artist, athlete, wife
The sailor has no time to fear the storm
  That frights the passenger for very life.

Light me to work, thou glorious daily sun;
Death, be a laggard till my work is done.

XI

Science

ACH day extends our knowledge, yet withal
    Gives us to know our ignorance the more.
    With ceaseless toil we climb one mountain
wall,
To find the mountain higher than before.
See yonder peak a school-boy now can scale?
    The man who climbed it first, climbed it alone!
Now from its very summit we can hail
    A ring of virgin heights, before unknown.
There is no limit to the mind or soul;
    There is no bound to Man's great upward trend;
Then bravely through the boundless mighty whole
    Extend we power and knowledge, ever extend.

Thus every day may Man still higher rise,
To find still wider visions greet his eyes.

XII

Art

THE foundry's glow pierced night and murk and
    mist ;
      Two strong, lithe flames leapt up into the air,
Then bent to one another, and then kissed.
  The soul of Man would choke in dull despair
Were not some instinct in him, whereby he
  To other men that soul's cry might impart.
When Man's creative force grows full and free,
  Becomes most human, then we call it " Art."
In vain the critic seeks with rules to bind it,
  Saying " It must be moral,"—" Must obey
The laws of beauty ; " spite of all we find it
  Free as the winds which go their wilful way.

Art is your brother's need of speech to you ;
Let but that speech to his own heart be true.

XIII

Time and Friendship

TIME is an Ocean, strewn with many wrecks;
   The child sits by its edge, and shouts with joy
   Across its wide expanse, and never recks
That Titan's dangerous strength, whom he'll employ
   To overflow his trenches in the sand.
Each wave in turn he orders to retreat
   And it obeys; leaving the yellow strand
With shells less dainty than his little feet.

   Time and the Sea are pastimes to the child;
And when he reaches Man's prerogative,
   And knows how both are wanton, cruel, wild,
He minds him still the pleasures they can give.

O friend, O comrade, Time hath given me
The joy of my full friendship unto thee.

c

XIV

Man and Fate

EN as a little boy with saucy lip,
   Who with pert words and deeds provoking
      stands,
Stirring some much-tried dame to chase and grip
   And trounce the lode-stone of her wrathful hands,
So Man tempts Fortune. Though her smile be kind,
   He will not rest content, but with rash mood
And graceless flouting of her friendly mind
   He goads the goddess till he flies, pursued
By her aroused ire; him soon she seizes
   And on the ivory tablets makes her score,
The tally of her rage; but when time eases
   His smart, he is no wiser than before.

Lives there a man or lad or little boy
Who doth not revel in such dangerous joy?

XV

Tears

TEARS, fears and doubtings, anguish of the
  soul,
    Ye are not absent, nor shall ever be ;
Long, long as Man with this sweet Earth shall roll,
  Still shall he blend pale grief with ecstasy.
Proud-humble Man, in his sad-glad estate,
  With varying emotion rounds his days ;
Loving, yet often blundering with his mate,
  Tender at heart-deep, e'en when anger sways.
As full of contradictions as of pluck ;
  Most foolish always when most logic claiming ;
Boasting of reason when most passion-struck ;
  Yet dear beyond all praising and all blaming !

Hope shines behind the blackest of our fears ;
Our joys are made the brighter by our tears.

XVI

Contrition

CONSCIOUS of many sins, denying none,
       Penitent, bowed before mine own ideals
       As one who 'gainst them many things hath
   done
   That should not have been done; cut by the wheels,
The knife-edge wheels of mine own Juggernaut;
   Bared before God, and by mine own soul scourged,
Yet in my very anguish comes the thought
   That I shall sin again when thereto urged
By mine own wantonness; and this concept
   Gives me not shame alone, but some strange sense
Of triumph; as if sin's wild tempest swept
   Man's life to heights more grand and. more intense.

The fullest grain hath not the least of bran;
Sin if thou must: but sin thou like a MAN.

XVII

Divination

THE Priest of old, red-handed, stern of eye,
Into the vitals of the victim slain,
Peered, and each quiver noted, greedily;
Thus, knowledge of Man's fate he claimed to gain.
We have made progress. Victims of to-day
Are not on ruthless altars reft of life;
Man's greed, lust, cruelty he must allay
By private wiles, and not by priestly knife.
The end's the same. The sweated, whipped, down-trodden,
(Like her on whom alone falls double shame)
Though harlot, pauper, criminal, drink-sodden,
All silently the old grim truth proclaim :—

Man's fate and future quick and quivering lies
In the bared entrails of the sacrifice.

XVIII

Despair and Brotherhood

INTO the dreadest cave of unbelief
    I will descend with thee, if thou dost suffer
    And find'st no comfort for thy bitter grief;
  I will curse God with thee, with curses rougher
Than thou dar'st use thyself; if thou'lt despair,
  And wilt not listen to my words of hope
I'll despair with thee; every pang to share
  Of dungeon, pillory, scourge, rack and rope.
If Hell there be, that Hell we all must enter,
  Brothers together, Christ by Judas' side;
Upon thy heart, my heart must ever centre;
  We are conjoined, as bridegroom unto bride.

Then when thou seest what brothers all men are,
Comes there not to thy dark a little star?

LIFE IN INSTANCES

XIX

Farm Life

THE homely farm, well-built of warm red stone,
    The dignified old farmer and his wife;
    The farmer's sons, for stalwart manhood
  known;
The daughters, with their busy, thrifty life,
Chaste, cheery maids, well fit for wifehood's vows,
  These rule the picture. To the farm-yard turn;
Here's healthy, fertile stock. The patient cows,
  Absolute subjects to their monarch stern;
The dull dependent sheep, the untiring dog;
  The baby pigs, with silky skins and fair,
The sow with beauteous teats, the lustful hog;
  The merry foal and docile, shapely mare.

Reigning o'er all is Man's commanding brain;
Yet behind all, the plenteous grass and grain.

XX

Dog and Wolf

THE wind-swept prairie onward rolls and melts
        In the far sky. The herds are breeding,
            thriving ;
Keen dogs with faithful hearts 'neath shaggy pelts
    Keep the grim wolf from his unholy living.
Ceaseless the feud between these kindred foes ;
    Yet by the mysteries of beating hearts,
There are dog-Juliets, and wolf Romeos,
    Whose wanton and forbid caress imparts
Such a wild splendid vigour to their litter,
    Such a new restless force to their strong brood
As makes us wonder which is really fitter,
    To be part wild, or to be all too good.

Dog, Wolf, and Man their own set parts fulfil,
Their small wills merging in Life's Infinite Will.

XXI

Big Ships and Small

ALL in a happy mood of holiday,
  I and my comrade dear, my boy of nine,
    Went forth upon a boat that steamed its way
  Warily, in a broken, salt-drenched line
Down a broad firth where waves with winds contended.
  How the boy laughed at every toss and pitch !
A bath of sea-spray seemed to him "just splendid;"
  Each quake, each risk of sandbank he made rich
With laughter ; merry while the others grumble
  "The skipper is not qualified"—"The boat
Is mere old metal"—"How her engines rumble !"
  The master steers his course, nor cares a groat.

We love big ships ; but he too makes his mark
Who brings to port his battered, clumsy barque.

An Art Circle

CTING and inter-acting on each other ;
    Speaking and inter-speaking, each to each ;
    Linked in their lives as brother unto brother,
  Oft with fraternal bluntness in their speech,
Thus live the circle that I know so well.
  They grind each other's art to finer edge
As mutual hopes they rouse, spur, damp and quell ;
  To help and hinder is their privilege ;
And both the help and hindrance make for goal.
  A varied diet doth our spirit need ;
Good, bad, praise, blame . . . . behind all grows the soul.
  Hail to the circle ; Comrades all, God-speed !

Though only one might climb the peak of fame,
The names of all should still stand near his name,

XXIII

Beethoven

MUCH more than Music, Ludwig, didst thou
  send us;
      Thine art, but also thine own self the gift;
Behind thy haunting strains, the power tremendous
  Of rich, strong art, we feel the grand uplift
Of that swift mighty spirit that explored
  For us all depths and heights of joy and woe;
Who gave to us his soul's great, priceless hoard
  Sun-like, to warm us with pervading glow.
He wore himself in wrestling with the intense;
  He gave his body, and he gave his blood.
We bathe in his emotion, sheer, immense;
  Rise pure, strong, glad, from that re-newing flood.

Great art demands a great life interwoven;
Great manhood taught great music to Beethoven.

Town Life

NEAR where a river merges in the sea
    I stroll and crunch the pebbles 'neath my feet,
    Noting their infinite variety,
The miles they must have travelled, here to meet
A thousand diff'rent geologic stages
    Their multi-colored products here compare
Where granite from the pre-historic ages
    Jostles odd chips of modern earthenware !
Ribbons of fading seaweed cling to some,
    And slacken not their hold, though slowly dying.
The Ocean's storm and scour and swirl and strum
    Have ground, then tossed them where they now are
      lying.

A town is nothing but a pebbly strand
Where men are flung by Fate's capricious hand.

On a Poster

JUST a mere poster stuck upon a wall,
  And yet it needs must ravish our attention;
  These are its words :—" I will stick up for all!"
O what a rare and beautiful contention!
Censorious folk, here passing, should be struck,
  Like king Belshazzar, in a guilty sweat;
Have we condemned our brothers, run amuck
  In scandal 'mid foes, friends and neighbours, yet
Have our own lives been just as kin to shame?
  Have we traced guilty lusts in others' eyes
Forgetting that our lids veil equal blame?
  " I will stick up for all." 'Tis good; 'tis wise.

Poster, my thanks. I'll own my heart beats quicker,
Though thou art but a pun of our bill-sticker.

At a Railway Station

LIFE with romance is full and brimming over ;
　　Each hour, each moment hath its thrill and cue;
　　Full of sweet bloom is every field of clover,
And honey-loving creatures search it through.
Look deep ; you'll find romance in every place. . . .
　　Yon railway-lad, built like a Greek Apollo,
Casts eager looks at that fair lady's face ;
　　His careless grace her furtive glances follow. . . .
She's rich, he's poor, all's over ; but that glance
　　Is not forgotten ; life is richer for it.
Our homespun's shot with threads of such romance ;
　　Our mind's a hive ; with honey sweet we store it.

Rosy romance our larger life is filling ;
And with her scent our passing breaths are thrilling.

LIFE'S WOMEN

D

XXVII

Woman

CREATIVE mystery; Man's ecstasy;
    Highest and lowliest, handmaiden and Queen;
    Saviour and sinner; life's epitome;
  Wildest of wild things, calmest of serene.
Primitive Man two tasks hath first essayed :—
  To bend both Fire and Woman to his will.
Greater and greater progress Man hath made,
  Yet Fire and Woman both defy him still !
The glow o' the hearth means home and all home joys;
  The burning house fills stricken hearts with terror;
The forest fire first kisses, then destroys;
  The beacon saves the wanderer from his error.

O Man ! When wilt thou learn to understand
That Fire and Woman still out-match thy hand ?

XXVIII

Marriage

LOVE thee ; 'tis a message old and sweet ;
 The older, still the sweeter, O my love.
  Thou lovest me ; this utterance, dear, repeat ;
Tireless the iteration of our love.
I need thee to perfect my manly force ;
 Is not that need a beauteous loving token ?
Thou needest me ; thy womanly life-course
 In me completes ; our lives in halves were broken
Were we to part. But while thus far is good,
 Our bonny babes are our best, foremost blessing ;
These from our love draw their strong vital food ;
 These to our virgin hearts gave mandates pressing.

The World gains men because I so love thee ;
Our love and joy both serve Eternity.

XXIX

Home

THE wilful plucky manhood of the father,
 Made greater, purer by the power of love;
 The winsome faithful wifehood of the mother,
 Made deeper, grander by the spell of love;
These three dimensions, length and breadth and height,
 Build up the home, and build it true and square.
The joyful, busy day and fragrant night
 Pour blessings down; and lovely things are there,
Toys, baby-cots, and boys' and girls' young laughter;
 The home is thus the fitting breeding place
For women, men and heroes; Love, the grafter,
 Of soft-rose upon wild-rose, works this grace.

In sweetest home we nestle ere our birth;
May we as sweetly lie in Mother Earth!

XXX

Passion

LOVE is not tame, nor birth; the fields in spring
  Glow with a rapture that's expressed in beauty;
  Unto conception comes no living thing
Unless some live spark fires the needful duty
That brings light out of darkness, life from fate;
  For virtue knows more throb and thrill than vice.
Keen is the fierce flash in the eyes of hate;
  With beating heart the gamester throws the dice;
But love, with all its magic faith hot glowing,
  And visions high of passionate purity,
Is still the greatest force of life's bestowing,
  Is still its maddest, sanest ecstasy.

Spirit of Man, tense be thy mortal striving;
No blasphemy of tameness mar thy living!

XXXI

A Working Woman

SHE'S down upon her knees; her body leaning
   Part on one hand, while swift the other goes
   With bold sure strokes about her doorstep-
cleaning;
  Absorbed in labour, she. Her swinging pose
Attracts our glance. To beauty's ballroom figure
  She lays no claim. Her bosom's matronly;
Her flanks and quarters have a buxom vigour;
  A strong ripe wench. Her open face, clear eye,
Are honest. On her shapely fore-arm, bare,
  We see tattooed in letters firm and bold
"True love to Thomas Clarke." We gladly share
  The bliss that frank avowal doth unfold.

The world needs lives so simple, strong and straight;
Joy and brave babes be thine, from thy staunch mate.

XXXII

Wantons

WHETHER we think of her whose beauty stands
    Displayed in Troy's fierce frame of gold
and red;
Or of that queen who, at her cousin's hands,
    Paid both for Darnley's death and Bothwell's bed;
Or of Nile's empress, Antony's death-rapture;
    Or, in our time, of that dark royal bride
Who, paying the grim price of sin and capture,
    Wrecked the stern Zulu nation when she died;
Whether 'tis public or 'tis private case,
    Still may we see the drawn and writhing prey
At wanton beauty's dainty gallows-place;
    Hold her who can and will, escape who may.

All men have known her since the world began;
God made her; I'll not judge her; I'm a man.

XXXIII

A Quiet Maid

IN the swift railway train she sat and knitted,
　　Changing its rush to peace. Her mouth and
　　eyes
Were soft and true; her well-marked figure fitted
　　For all that Woman's fullest life implies.
Silent and busy, and to me unknown,
　　Yet clearly was her worth as real and modest
As was her bosom's beauty, veiled, yet shown
　　By favour of a sigh, though trimly bodiced.
So ripe for life, with all her daintiness;
　　So dainty-sweet, throughout her working mood,
Can a man look on such and not confess
　　The up-lifting charm of quiet womanhood?

Deft maid, mine eyes were glad in noticing
Upon thy hand a neat engagement ring.

XXXIV

A Man's Woman

IN every mood love should be known by thee
The whole of Womanhood glow in thy veins.
Be Eve of Paradise, yet Eve when she
Was drunk with learning of love's needs and pains.
Love thou with softness, raptly, tenderly,
Yet know swift love that burns for satisfaction;
Love as all women can, unselfishly,
Yet with primeval hunger of attraction.
Chaste as Lucrece unto thy marriage vows,
Yet show thy mate such passion as consumed
The vitals of maimed Potiphar's fierce spouse;
To love with all thy being be thou doomed.

He who made human love hath made it thus.
Deny not truth. Pray for thyself—and us.

XXXV

The Home Woman

HER lips are love; her bosom, peace; her eyes,
   Slow to condemn, are quick to see and aid;
   Her voice can both delight and sympathize,
But not complain; nor would it e'er persuade
Save in such things as Woman knoweth best.
   Laughter she loves, and little children run
Unto her motherly arms and fragrant breast.
   Ev'ry man likes her; but she chooses one
For that full love that is beyond all other;
   His is the sacred right of fatherhood
Unto her babes. She is a happy mother,
   Looks on young life and sees that it is good.

She could not be a saint if saints be cold;
Love thrills her bosom to its inmost fold.

XXXVI

A Kiss

TWO rosy apples, hanging from one stalk;
  And yet betwixt the two a gleam of fire;
  Two round-backed ponies, with a stately walk,
Linked to the chariot of just desire;
And when the master, stern, applies the goad,
  With sweet confusion yet with perfect grace
The merry ponies haste their loving load.
  Look now around; this is the holy place
Where love and faith and triumph send deep roots
  Into the strong Earth's recreative womb.
Taste of the tree; enjoy her juicy fruits,
  While the soul's wings are growing, plume by plume.

The fertile flow'r sweet honey must exhale;
The fertile soul hath joy that shall not fail.

LIFE'S CHILDREN

Creative Love

 AM the fuel and the fire art thou;
 THOU art the fuel and the fire am I;
 Thus each in turn knows the deep need of
now
 Which serves dim centuries of bye-and-bye.
Thus out of passion, life, and out of life,
 Passion again; and ever on and on
The stream of souls flows to the mingled strife
 And triumph of the Universe; out-shone
Are all the suns of yesterday, whose light
 Pales before ours, as ours in turn will pale.
The upward path, the ever noble fight,
 The long-drawn victory that cannot fail.

O love creative! Thy fierce majesty
Towers to the heights of ideality.

XXXVIII

Motherhood

DUTY and rapture in creative power;
  Achievement and delight in self-same guise.
  Eternity was wrapped into an hour,
And Sex became co-eval with the Skies,
Then Life new dawned; O sweetest of content!
  So much encompassed in so little space;
The babe-life, race-life, mother-life, all blent,
  Man's destiny in one dear baby-face.
Joy of the flow'r, because it is the seed,
  Joy of the flesh because it is the soul,
Joy of our blood and spirit which thus speed
  Through distant generations countless roll.

" My bosom's babe," saith Mother-ecstasy,
" My might and wisdom are summed up in thee."

XXXIX

Birth

THE new-born babe utters his plaintive wail .
   Another life to taste life's mystery !
   Now fresh begins the never-ending tale,
Earth's marvel, life's increase, love's potency.
Thou, little one, wilt count the starry skies
   Though now thou scarcely seest thy hands of silk ;
For thee the Ocean tides shall fall and rise ;
   To-day thine only care is flow of milk
Unto thy mother's breasts. Some day again,
   Weary of wisdom and philosophy,
A woman's breast shall ease thee of thy pain,
   A woman's love mother a child for thee.

The World rolls on, still seeking what is best ;
The babe still finds it—at his mother's breast.

To a Mother

THIS beauteous happiness of baby-life,
    Grown from thy loving essence, comes to thee,
    And all the world with joy and hope is rife.
The future, present, past—eternity—
Merge in this sweet wee being. All we are,
    And were, and will be, centres now in her.
For her the earth bears fruit, and every star
    Peeps from its height, its deep faith to aver
In baby-life, brought forth anew to-day ;
    For Cosmos in new-birth still finds its joy.
"Creation is all one," the star-worlds say ;
    The miracle of birth shall never cloy.

"Creation is all one," the star-worlds say ;
    Each birth is Nature's happy holiday.

XLI

To all Mothers

THE mother hath essential sacredness,
    Whatever her condition or degree;
    Repaying birth by birth in mortal stress,
Her mite she gives unto eternity.
Be she the source of many a healthy child,
    Or one; or of rough louts or weaklings cherished,
Be she or wise or unwise, stern or mild
    Or blindly foolish, still her sap hath nourished
Infinite fate with infinite devotion;
    Life's vehicle, e'en though her eyes be bound
And her hands tied; kindling our tense emotion,
    And with our wreath of thorns and lilies crowned.

"Life and more life," cries Earth, "life overflowing."
Responsively the mother-heart is glowing.

XLII

Ebb and Flow

MAN hath a thousand ways in which to slay,
    Yet Motherhood repairs the waste of all;
    Man kills for pomp or folly, lust, hate, play,
For every twisted passion of the fall,
And Motherhood must still the waste repair.
    Commerce, peace, leisure, equally can kill,
And Woman of Man's death hath caused her share;
    All causes join, Death's harvest to fulfil.
But Cupid comes, with lissom double bow;
    His merciless keen dart he makes us taste;
Love's poignant pangs lay slothful pleasure low,
    And busy motherhood repairs all waste.

The gods of Death brag boldly on their course,
Yet little feeble Cupid hath more force.

The Child

F Earth had ne'er a child, men would despair.
　　Not only would endeavour lose its goal,
　　And Earth the loveliest thing that breathes
　the air ;
Greatest of all the loss unto the soul.
It is the child who teaches us to know,
　By its great innocence and trifling sin,
How lovable is Man. However low
　Man falls, the image of the child within
Bids pause our condemnation ; for him, too,
　A mother suffered, wept, rejoiced and strove.
His wanton sins himself the most shall rue ;
　His greatest need is still the need of love.

Unto the child to teach us it is given
How we ourselves partake the grace of Heaven.

XLIV

My Babes

DEARER than rest, wherein each tired nerve glows;
   Dearer than mighty hills or salty sea;
   Dearer than music's haunting after-close;
  Dearer than all, my babies unto me.
Dearer than e'en thy kisses' rhythm, deep;
  Dearer than e'en thy message when afar;
Dearer than e'en thine eyes, in mellow sleep;
  Dearer than all, our merry babies are.
All that I have of good, may they inherit;
  All that I have of bad, may they set right;
All I have sought and failed in, may they bear it
  Up to where Triumph shines in starry height.

Transcendent glimpses of Eternity,
Babies who play about their father's knee

XLV

Justification

" AND next whom will you sit?" the mother said
     The night before the party was to be.
     Her eight-year-old boy raised his pretty head:
" Next the most loneliest, Mummy dear," said he.
God bless thee, little boy, who knows so well
     By loving instinct, all we need to know.
If in the future Heaven awaits, or Hell,
     Still by thy side I'd be content to go,
Face any judgment, bow to any law,
     For all my grievous sins suffer, atone,
Admit my littleness before God's Awe
     And just put one plea forward, one alone :—
" That boy was mine, who said with so much grace
     " By the most loneliest, Mummy, be my place."

XLVI

Child Wonder

THE wonder of the child may I still keep;
   His hope, faith, gaiety, surprise and love;
   Laugh as he laughs, and as he weepeth weep;
His purity of heart, all gifts above,
Strive I to hold as long as I have breath.
   Thus may I live by his example bright,
And sleep at last on th' mother-breast of Death
   With a tired sigh, as one who fears not night.
O, dear-loved child, that all prevading Force
   That made the awe-swept mystery of the womb
And set thy merry blood in sweet, pure course,
   Guideth aright our mortal birth, life, doom.

Lo, in this faith and joy, with praise and prayer,
I kiss my little darling's golden hair.

LIFE'S FAITH

The Twofold Life

 TENSE, pent passion of the nightingale,
     Throb upon throb, brave dreams made living
       song,
Thus in the night may burning thoughts assail
  Our womb-like spirits with enforcement strong.
But when the sun shines brightly o'er the meads,
  The skylark, with rapt voice of ecstasy,
Hymns the delights of daily hopes and needs,
  Th' eternal joy of life's mad mystery.
O singers twain, to you I ever hark,
  Life's double aspect richly ye recite;
Superb strong moody passion of the dark,
  Grand restless ceaseless energy of the light.

The babe sucks at two breasts, lovely at each;
Sing, birds; suck, babes; I ponder what ye teach.

XLVIII

Is Life Enough ?

"OUR life is not enough, nor could be, ever."
    Such is the cry the striving spirit makes
    In restless dreams of searching, high endeavour.
Then straightway on the world the spirit wakes
And with superb activities makes way,
    Destroying and renewing and destroying ;
Gaining new dreams each night, new light each day,
    Cloyed with the world, with striving never cloying.
A noble discontent is still the sign
    Of Man's unceasing fight for betterment ;
Yet, having that, we still will not resign
    The splendid force of our superb content.

He who knows one mood only, nothing knows ;
God gave a wealth of petals to the rose.

XLIX

Not Sinless, We

NOT gilded butterflies, to sun our wings
    In a tame perfect world ; not passion-free,
    Not sinless, not all good. Our primal springs
Of action blend much good, much evil ; we
Are not with known years numbered, nor are come
    From one seed only : in our blood still rife
The blood of things with fangs. We are the sum
    Of all Earth's vast experiments in life.
Our mem'ries date from prehistoric days ;
    There countless myriads of impressions jostle ;
We are their sublimate, and know the ways
    Whereby fierce brute becomes divine apostle.

Not one of our blood's heirlooms can we spare ;
Not less, but more sense-fulness be our share.

L

Understanding

WE search into the life which all men lead,
　　Its fervour, frenzy, folly, love and hate,
　　Its hours of baseness, yet its daily need
Of something higher than the highest state
The soul attains to; patiently we learn
　　The blackest and the whitest truths to know
About our kin; and from these truths discern
　　The brotherhood betwixt the high and low,
The vital promise that each human life
　　Breathes forth as truly as we know it lives;
Till the whole trend of our blind earthly strife
　　Clears to our eager dream-sight, ay, and gives
Assurance that the seers tell aright:—
　　The Fate of Man climbs slowly up the height.

LI·

Life is Enough

RINGED in by boundless possibilities,
　　With glad, full hearts we cry " Life is enough "
　　Each day is full of opportunities ;
In each encouragement and each rebuff
We find our striving gains an added zest.
　　The old hath still a friendly, well-known face ;
The spell remains of that which once hath blest ;
　　The New still finds its own inspiring place.
The round of life is joyous ; every sun
　　Doth rise upon a world both old and new ;
The thing to do ; the thing that's doing, done ;
　　The energy, life, hope of me and you.

Man is still made of sound courageous stuff ;
His glowing veins still sing " Life is enough."

All Pervading Poetry

THE living soil of life is fertilised
　　By sunshine of Man's joy, rain of his tears
　　No spot so bare but what some soul hath
prized
　Its hidden secret, blent with hopes and fears.
Each throb of life's a seed of the sublime;
　Thus with a poet's colour fervent glows
Each act, small, large, Christ-cross or Judas-crime.
　For every thrilling charm a lover knows
He finds at once a second and a third.
　The beauty of the wild-rose is complete;
But see, its juicy hips feed many a bird,
　New seeds grow warm within their entrails sweet

Not the eyes only, but the soul doth see;
The commonest things are filled with poetry.

LIII

Dreams

DREAMS that out-speed the patient pace of life
   Tell us the tale of wider life to come ;
    High-visioned Man, in his keen, restless strife
Ever extends his power and wisdom's sum.
Our nature is too large for our estate ;
   Slowly the flesh moves, swift the spirit dances ;
In dream-life we escape our mortal fate
   And then return to live, with brightened glances
And freshened strength, the life of every day.
   Full many dreams come true in our own time ;
And many more when Death hath calmed our clay ;
   And many more wait till their hour shall chime.

God's Universe hath Life close packed and teeming ;
Life ; fertile life ; prophetic life of dreaming.

LIV

Religion

FAITH, faith to the full, we know not how or why,
    Except that life is all made up of faith
    That glows, world-lustrous, from the Starry sky;
The planets all obey, the heart obey'th.
Faith, faith to the full; because the mountain-peak
    Utters grand messages to headlong clouds;
Because lake, woodland, sea, in splendour speak,
    And dead men's mouths so calmly kiss their shrouds;
Because all women's breasts are richly dight
    With faith and music, love and constancy;
The infant smiles when he doth see the light;
    All great things give us joy, right graciously.

Life's meaning, faith's full word, I do not know;
I know the life and faith with which I glow.

LV

Joy

THE blood is liquid joy that bathes the brain,
   Warming and gaining warmth from sense and soul.
   The game of life, whether we lose or gain,
  Is all superb; accept it, frankly, whole,
Substract no part, but revel to the full
  In its completeness; scum and sin have place;
Out of manure grow roses; Nature's rule
  Doth not despise or cavil; our full grace,
Our manhood, womanhood, our weakness, force,
  Love, failure, happiness, our drama keen
Lives in the fullness of our life's fierce course,
  In our whole selves, the seen and the unseen.

GOD hath ordained you, Manhood, Womanhood;
JOY is your birth-right; Life is full and good.

LVI

Pantheism

LIFE is stark full of beauty and of force;
  Its throb and ecstasy are from that Power
  Which fills the wondrous All, and holds its
    course
Majestic in the planets, sweet in the flower.
All Nature is akin. Though we may be
  Mere breaths of Her immense and awful Will,
Yet moulded straight from God-touched clay are we
  Who compass so much good and so much ill,
So strong and weak and wilful and sublime.
  Thus in the Blend Supreme we have our part;
The shadow of God's truth; the toy of time;
  And yet the God-pulse beats with our weak heart.

Almighty God of all things! May we see
Forever our full harmony with Thee!

LIFE IS ENOUGH

POSTLUDE.

"LIFE IS ENOUGH."

NOTE.—This is designed so that it can immediately follow the Prelude, the two then forming a consistent whole.

Notes in brackets may be omitted with a view to simplification.

The Orchestral score of this Postlude may be borrowed from the Composer.

CPSIA information can be obtained
at www.ICGtesting.com
Printed in the USA
BVHW010908300821
615581BV00003B/177

9 781162 206066

DISCOVER TIMES
GREAT CITIES
Manchester

TOP LEFT: A MANCHESTER MILLWORKER, *c* 1935; CENTRE: TRIUMPHAL ARCH, TRAFFORD PARK, *c* 1910;
TOP RIGHT: CHILDREN IN THE MOUTH OF A REPLICA WHALE, BELLE VUE, 1955;
MAIN PICTURE: ST ANN'S SQUARE, 1905

ROBERT GIBB

MYRIAD
LONDON

THE CITY CENTRE

Mancunium, a Roman fort, was sited at the crossroads of some of the most strategic routes in Roman Britain. From this historic beginning the modern city of Manchester developed. The Industrial Revolution fuelled a tremendous growth in population and the city's fine Victorian architecture reflects its wealth and importance since that time

ABOVE: **MARKET STREET, 1895.** Horse-drawn trams ferry passengers to and from the busy city centre. Destinations include Alexandra Park, Brooks' Bar and Hyde Road. The pavements are heaving with shoppers and business people. Market Street was widened between 1822 and 1834 at a cost of £200,000.

ABOVE: **PICCADILLY, c 1910.** The final stages of the demolition of the Royal Infirmary that was built on this site in 1775. Part of the building, which still intact, is the accident room on Parker Street. The tower in the background is part of the Minshull Street law courts.

BELOW: **PICCADILLY GARDENS, 1936.** A view of the gardens from Portland Street looking towards Lewis's department store on the other side. The gardens were once a claypit until Lord Mosley donated the land for use as a public garden in the late 18th century.

ABOVE: **PICCADILLY, c 1890.** The Royal Infirmary on the right-hand side casts a dark shadow over Piccadilly. On the corner of Mosley Street stands the statue of Robert Peel, erected in 1856, which looks towards Oldham Street. This was Manchester's first outdoor statue financed by public subscription. Over £3,000 was collected within a week.

ABOVE: **EXCHANGE STATION AND CROMWELL'S STATUE**, *c* 1885. The imposing statue of Cromwell looks up Victoria Street. Erected in 1875, in 1968 it was moved to Wythenshawe Hall which, during the Civil War, the Roundhead troops used as a billet. Exchange Station was demolished in the mid 1980s and replaced by a car park.

BELOW: **MARKET STREET, 1953.** Crowds of shoppers throng the city centre dodging traffic on the corner of Cross Street, looking up towards Piccadilly in the distance. The Arndale Centre now occupies the left-hand side of Market Street from Burton's the tailors to Debenhams in the distance. When the Arndale was completed in 1979 it was the largest covered retail area in Europe.

ABOVE: **MANCHESTER CATHEDRAL, 1936.** The memorial service for the death of King George V (1910-1936) in Manchester Cathedral. The king had been a regular visitor to Manchester, particularly during the First World War and its aftermath. In 1934 he opened the new Central Library.

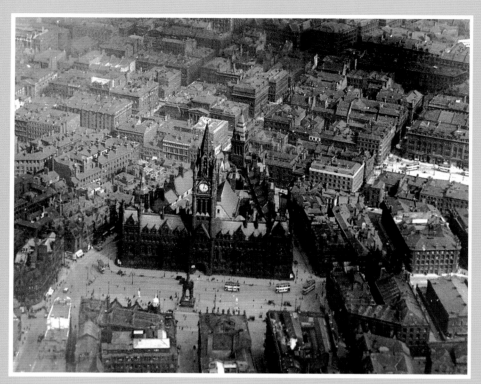

LEFT: **ALBERT SQUARE**, *c 1922*. An aerial view of the town hall and surrounding buildings. Albert Square and St Peter's Square are clearly visible.

BELOW LEFT: **ALBERT SQUARE**, *c 1950*. Manchester Town Hall dominates Albert Square. The skyline from the square has changed very little to this day.

BOTTOM LEFT: **THE ART GALLERY AND MOSLEY STREET, 1880.** A police officer stands at the junction of Princess Street and Mosley Street waiting to direct traffic. In the foreground is the Manchester Art Gallery. The building was designed by Charles Barry and opened in 1834; it has operated as the City Art Gallery since 1882.

BELOW: **SPRING GARDENS**, *c 1910*. A busy scene on the cobbled Spring Gardens outside the Post Office. In the background is the new Midland Bank in its final stages of completion. This huge Art Deco-style building is clad in white stone and was designed by Sir Edwin Luytens who also designed the cenotaph in St Peter's Square.

ABOVE: **SPRING GARDENS POST OFFICE,** *c* 1898. The central Post Office in Manchester employed hundreds of staff to deal with mail and telegraph post. Smart appearance was essential and all staff were required to dress in collar and tie.

ABOVE: **THE MANCHESTER GUARDIAN BUILDING,** *c* 1905. The original *Manchester Guardian* and *Manchester Evening News* building stood opposite the Exchange building on Cross Street. The papers were printed in the basement and then rushed over to horse-drawn carts for distribution. The ground floor contained the advertising department. In 1970 the papers moved from Cross Street to new offices in Deansgate. They had been written and printed at the Cross Street building since 1886.

LEFT: **MARKET STREET AND ITS JUNCTION WITH CROSS STREET,** 1914. Since the 13th century Market Street has been at the centre of the city's retail trade. The first horse-drawn omnibus service in Britain was started in 1824 between Pendleton and Market Street.

LEFT: **THE ASSIZE COURTS** *c* 1895. Begun in 1859 the Assize Courts were the first major work of Alfred Waterhouse (1830-1905) who also designed Manchester Town Hall and whose Gothic-style architecture is so important in the Manchester streetscape. Located close to Strangeways Prison, the courts were constructed at a cost of over £13,000. The statue of Moses, known as the lawgiver, stood over the entrance. The courts were badly damaged during the Blitz of 1940-41 and were subsequently demolished.

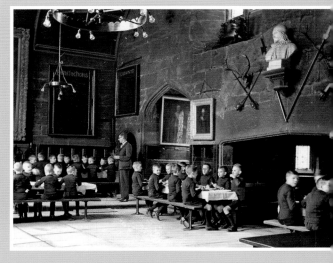

ABOVE: **MANCHESTER CENTRAL LIBRARY UNDER CONSTRUCTION, 1932.** Manchester was the first local authority to set up a public lending and reference library and the first library was opened in 1852 at the Hall of Science, Campfield (on the site of the current Air and Space Museum). The collection soon outgrew these premises and the architect E Vincent Harris (1876-1971) won an architectural competition to build the new Central Library and Town Hall extension. In 1930 the Prime Minister, Ramsay MacDonald, laid the foundation stone and in 1934 the new library was opened by King George V. At the time it was the largest public library in the country and it is still one of the busiest.

ABOVE: **CHETHAM'S SCHOOL, 1938.** Young boys in the dining hall of the famous school with its superb inglenook fireplace. This ancient manor house, which dates from 1421, is the most complete set of medieval buildings to survive in north-west England. It occupies the site of the manor house of Manchester which, together with the parish church (now the Cathedral), formed the core of the medieval town. It was saved from destruction in 1651 by Manchester cloth merchant Humphrey Chetham whose bequest allowed for renovation of the building and the establishment of a school to educate 40 poor children. In 1969 Chetham became a co-educational school for young musicians.

ABOVE: **DEANSGATE, 1900.** Deansgate was the home of many quality shops, businesses and services. The Old Picture Shop displayed its paintings outside to catch the eye of potential customers.

BELOW: An aerial view of the **DEANSGATE** district which clearly shows the City Exhibition Hall, St Matthew's and St John's churches, the Opera House, Sunlight House and, on the right, the LNER goods yard.

ABOVE: **KING STREET 1900.** Most of the property on King Street consisted of business or professional accommodation. Houses had been steadily demolished during the preceding years to make way for prestigious office buildings and banks. In the distance the Manchester Reform Club displays traces of its Gothic architecture. Built between 1870-1 by Edward Salomons, it was one of the largest purpose-built clubhouses outside London. A grand staircase runs the height of the building from the spacious entrance hall, and on the ground floor there are magnificent lavatories with marble washbasins.

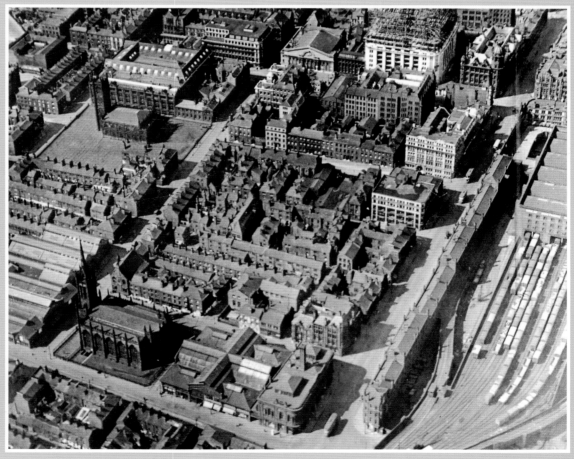

Transport

Manchester can lay claim to a clutch of British transport "firsts" — the first passenger railway line was the one from Manchester to Liverpool, served by the first passenger railway station at Liverpool Road. Barton Airport was the UK's first municipal airport and the Manchester Ship Canal was the first canal to link ocean-going ships to a British city

THE MANCHESTER SHIP CANAL stretches 36 miles from the southern shore of the Mersey estuary to within a mile of Manchester city centre. Opened in 1894, the canal was built to avoid the high cost of shipping goods through Liverpool Docks.

ABOVE: **TRAFFORD ROAD BRIDGE, 1894.** The Swing Bridge was one of seven bridges to span the canal. Built in 1892 by Butler and Co of Leeds, it was the smallest bridge on the canal but, at 1,800 tons, the heaviest. Just beyond the bridge is Pomona Dock.

RIGHT: **MANCHESTER SHIP CANAL, c 1890.** Salford dock number 7, on a misty day as a ship sets sail with a cargo bound for Liverpool.

ABOVE: **MANCHESTER SHIP CANAL, DRY DOCK, 1901.** The *Elswick Lodge* in dry dock having her hull repaired and painted. The two dry docks at Trafford Park were large enough to repair ships of all sizes including ocean-going liners.

ABOVE: **HORSE-DRAWN OMNIBUS, 1880.** Operating on the route from Cheadle to Manchester via Didsbury, this privately-owned carriage could carry up to 42 passengers bound for the city centre. Twelve people had to brave the elements by sitting on the open upper deck.

INSET: **TICKET COLLECTOR, 1917.** In the early part of the 20th century the Lancashire and Yorkshire Railway was one of the most heavily worked railway networks in the country and employed a small army of uniformed inspectors to check tickets.

BELOW: **MARKET STREET, 1930.** A line of passengers join the number 35 tram.

BOTTOM: **PICCADILLY BUS STATION, 1935.** Passengers wait patiently in the rain for the bus home.

ABOVE: **DEANSGATE, 1901.** A crowd of trackmen gather around the newly-laid St Mary's Gate junction on Deansgate — a vital part of the city's first electric-powered tramway from Albert Square to Cheetham Hill.

BELOW: **ALBERT SQUARE, 1901.** The official opening of the electric tramway on June 6 1901 was attended by thousands of spectators and officials, the crowds controlled by numerous police officers. Over 500 new trams were used between 1901 and 1903. The Queen's Road depot accommodated over half the vehicles and Hyde Road depot was built to house the balance.

ABOVE: **GAS GUZZLER, 1939.** This *Manchester Evening News* photograph from early on in the war is of the first car to be converted to run on gas. Nearly two decades on, Manchester citizens (above left) are still protesting about fuel rationing!

LEFT: **MINSHULL STREET, 1905.** The canal bridge next to the law courts undergoing repairs.

ABOVE: **PICCADILLY STATION, 1960.** Manchester-bound visitors arrive by train at the newly-modernised station, rebuilt to accommodate modern electric train services to London. The original London Road station was re-named Manchester Piccadilly after this facelift.

RIGHT: **STEAM TRAIN, STALYBRIDGE, 1966.** Steam trains like this one which operated on the trans-Pennine route to Leeds were largely phased out in the 1960s to make way for diesel and electric-powered stock.

ABOVE: **MANCHESTER AIRPORT, JULY 1930.** Airport dignitaries await the arrival of Lady Bailey, one of the pioneering figures in women's aviation, for the King's Cup air race around England. Established by King George V as an incentive for the development of British light aircraft and engine design, the event was watched by over 30,000 people.

ABOVE: **CHAT MOSS AERODROME, 1931.** Film actress Frances Day poses with a De Havilland DH 60 X Moth with the emblem of Manchester Airport painted on the fuselage.

RIGHT: **MANCHESTER AIRPORT, 1950.** In the golden age of air travel there were very few passengers. Compared with today, when more than 150,000 passengers a year pass through the departure lounge, this photograph of the main reception area at Ringway shows how few people travelled by air at this time.

ABOVE: **MANCHESTER AIRPORT, 1932.** The City Council wanted to be the first in Britain to have a licensed airfield, and Barton was chosen to replace an earlier airfield at Alexandra Park when the landowner refused to sell the site. Barton opened in 1930 and included a control tower and large hangar. With only a grass runway it soon became unsuitable for larger aircraft and an area south of Manchester was earmarked for development. Named Ringway, it took three years to construct and opened in June 1938.

Heavy Industry

Manchester has long been at the heart of Britain's transport manufacturing industry – particularly the building of aircraft and locomotives. The establishment of these highly skilled enterprises brought in its wake a network of support industries to the area

ABOVE: **AN AERIAL VIEW OF MOSTON, 1935.** The electronics giant Ferranti moved to the north-west from London tempted by lower land costs and wages. Pioneering work on the development of computers — including the first basic computer known as "the baby" —- was done at Moston in collaboration with the University of Manchester; the Ferranti archive was based there until 1990.

ABOVE: **HULME, 1907.** The first car built by Rolls Royce in 1904 parked in Cooke Street, Hulme. This car sold for £395 when it was built — today it is valued at approximately £250k. The famous radiator badge, known as the "Spirit of Ecstasy", was introduced in 1911 and was based on Eleanor Thornton, the secretary and mistress of Lord Montague of Beaulieu, a Rolls Royce customer.

ABOVE: **CROSSLEY ELECTRIC BATTERY VEHICLE, 1935.** Francis and William Crossley formed their famous company in 1867. Development work on these electric-powered vehicles stopped before the Second World War, when the firm shifted production to the manufacture of military vehicles.

LEFT: **OLD TRAFFORD,** *c* 1920. A car is re-fuelled on the forecourt of H&J Quick, an authorised Ford dealer.

RIGHT: **MANCHESTER SHIP CANAL, 1929.** Locomotives from the Beyer Peacock Railway Works (known locally as Gorton Tank) waiting to be loaded onto ships for delivery around the world and (below) being craned into position. The works at Gorton Foundry on Railway Street began production in 1854 and manufactured more than 8,000 locomotives. The works closed in 1966; today the buildings are used as a depot for Manchester Corporation, although some of the railway lines can still be seen.

BOTTOM: **THE CROSSLEY WORKS IN OPENSHAW, 1934.** This important workshop employed many skilled craftsmen from coach builders to coach painters. Here we see skilled men painting motor bus bodies before they are fitted to the chassis.

ABOVE: **CLOVER MILL, ROCHDALE, 1952.** The great fire at the mill on June 5 1952 caused over £1m worth of damage. More than 250 firemen battled for nine hours to extinguish the blaze, thought to have started when a blow lamp exploded in the basement.

THE COTTON CONNECTION

Manchester's wealth was founded on cotton. Many of the grandees of the industry had radicalism in their bones — not only did they fight to repeal the hated Corn Laws but, in the wake of the Peterloo Massacre of 1821, they set up their own newspaper — the Manchester Guardian. Other newspapers followed and soon virtually every national newspaper had an office in the city

BELOW: **THE OFFICES OF THE DAILY HERALD, OXFORD STREET, c 1930.** Sub-editors prepare copy before the paper goes to press. Launched in 1911, the *Daily Herald* moved to its Oxford Street premises in 1930. This radical title was set up in the aftermath of a printworkers strike and became the voice of the labour movement – although it was highly critical of the Labour government of Ramsay MacDonald. It was the first newspaper to sell 2m copies a day and the only paper to fully support the suffragettes in their fight for the vote.

ABOVE: **ANCOATS, c 1939.** Reels of paper arrive on wagons at the *Daily Express* building in Ancoats. This impressive glass structure was designed by Sir Owen Williams and built in 1939. It is one of the first examples of the Modernist style in Manchester. The triple height rooms on the ground floor were built to accommodate the printing presses.

LEFT AND RIGHT: **THE CROSS STREET OFFICES OF THE MANCHESTER GUARDIAN AND MANCHESTER EVENING NEWS.** The papers and their printworks were based at Cross Street from 1886 until the move, in 1970, to Deansgate, where many important editorial and advertising departments are currently located.

The photograph (right) shows a crane outside the Cross Street building as the papers prepare to move in August 1970; the offices were finally demolished in 1972.

MANCHESTER COTTON MILL, *c* 1935. Cotton manufacture developed in Lancashire due to an extensive labour force and a plentiful supply of soft water. In the 1830s approximately 85% of all cotton manufactured worldwide was produced in Lancashire.

LEFT AND ABOVE: **WOMEN TEXTILE WORKERS.** Working alongside men in the mills and earning a wage meant that Lancashire women became known for their independence and self-reliance, and many campaigned for radical causes — from votes for women to equal pay. The woman pictured here is working as a "beamer" or checker. Notice how carefully she is examining the fabric for any faults.

ABOVE: **FABRIC PRODUCTION** involved turning raw cotton, which was usually imported from the USA via Liverpool, into finished cloth. Many of the hot and dirty activities were performed by women, who were overseen by male machine operators. The aristocrats of the cotton industry were the men known as "mule-spinners" – they earned a "family wage" and their wives did not have to go out to work.

ABOVE: **THE SHIRLEY INSTITUTE, DIDSBURY, 1936.** The Victorian house north of the laboratories was described by Sir Nikolaus Pevsner as "the grandest of all Manchester mansions". Named The Towers it was originally owned by John Edward Taylor, the proprietor of the *Manchester Guardian*. In 1874 it was bought by the engineer Daniel Adamson and in 1882 a meeting was held there at which the decision to set up the Manchester Ship Canal was taken. In 1920 The Towers was purchased by the British Cotton Industry Research Association, and named the Shirley Institute after the daughter of a Stockport MP, William Greenwood. The first purpose-built laboratories at the institute were opened in 1922 by the Duke of York.

LEISURE — WHIT WALKS AND BELLE VUE

In its heyday, Belle Vue — "the showground of the world" — was the greatest outdoor attraction in the United Kingdom. As late as the 1960s it was the country's largest inland amusement park and the most important provincial zoo

ABOVE: AN AERIAL PHOTOGRAPH OF THE GIANT BELLE VUE SITE, 1922. In the foreground the caterpillar and "bobs" and in the distance the boating lake in the centre of which was the famous Jennison clock tower. It was named after John Jennison who started the park in 1836 and was demolished in 1949. A windmill was erected in its place. In 1963 the lake was drained and filled in after the water supply from the Stockport branch canal came to an end.

RIGHT: BELLE VUE KEEPER, 1920. The monkey terrace was added to the side of the elephant house in the late 1890s and was an extremely popular attraction for children, especially at tea-party time.

BELOW LEFT: BELLE VUE, *c* 1900. Among the many attractions the figure of eight and the toboggan rides dominate the skyline. As newer rides eventually became more popular and maintenance costs rose, so the "bobs" were demolished.

LEFT: BELLE VUE, 1946. Visitor numbers exceeded all expectations, even in the aftermath of the war. In the crowd servicemen can be seen, enjoying a day out while home on leave. The caterpillar was the most popular ride of the park and at peak times an hour's wait was quite common.

ABOVE: **CAESAR'S PALACE** has had many uses throughout its life, first as a restaurant, then a hotel and lastly as a public house. The front elevation of the building collapsed in 1980 and the rest of the building was demolished.

TOP: **CHILDREN IN THE MOUTH OF A REPLICA WHALE, BELLE VUE, 1955**. Known as "Willie", the real whale was housed in an aquarium in the children's zoo.

ABOVE: **BELLE VUE, 1903**. Buffalo Bill and his wild west circus were regular visitors to Belle Vue. The show included portrayals of a buffalo hunt, an Indian attack and even Custer's last stand.

LEFT: **MARKET STREET**, *c* 1950. The Church of England Whit Sunday walk parades down Market Street. Whit Walks took place on Whitsuntide — the seventh Sunday after Easter — when children carrying posies and banners paraded from their local churches to the city centre. It was customary for children to wear a new set of clothes for the occasion. The walks were watched by thousands of people who gathered along the pavements in front of the shops, bringing the city centre to a standstill.

SPORT

Sport and leisure have always been a fundamental part of life in Manchester, the home of two famous top-class football teams as well as Lancashire Cricket Club. Athletes and supporters from all over the globe come to the city to participate in and enjoy sport

RIGHT: **OLD TRAFFORD, 1930.** Founded in 1892, for its first nine years Manchester United Football Club was called Newton Heath. The team shown here finished 22nd in league division 1 with 22 points.

BELOW: **FA CUP FINAL, WEMBLEY, 1934.** Sam Cowan, Manchester City captain, accepts the trophy after the team's victory over Portsmouth in 1934. Sam Cowan was appointed player-manager at Mossley in 1937. He died in 1964 aged 62 after collapsing whilst refereeing a charity cricket match in aid of wicket-keeper Jim Parks.

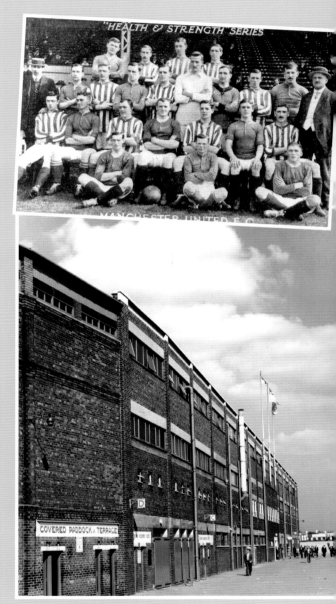

ABOVE: **MAINE ROAD, 1950.** Bert Trautmann, City's famous German goalkeeper, is swamped by autograph-hunters outside the Maine Road ground. Trautmann spent part of the war at a POW camp in Ashton and was brought to the club in 1949 by manager John Thomson — a highly controversial move which sparked a demonstration of 40,000 people on the city streets. Trautmann eventually won the hearts and minds of the Maine Road fans and was awarded the OBE in 2004.

ABOVE: **OLD TRAFFORD, 1959.** United moved from their old ground at Bank Street, Clayton to a brand-new stadium at Old Trafford. For its da Old Trafford was a state of the art facility with terracing on three sides and a covered main stand with seating. It was designed by the famous Scottish architect Archibald Leitch, who built many other football stadiums including Hampden Park. Old Trafford was badly bomb-damaged during the Second World War and United played their home games at Maine Road from 1946-49.

RIGHT: **OLD TRAFFORD CRICKET GROUND, 1957.** The Warwick Road ground hosted a three-day match that summer between Lancashire and the West Indies. The Windies won by nine wickets.

INSET: **LANCASHIRE WOMAN CRICKETER, 1938.** The history of women's cricket stretches back at least 250 years: the first recorded match in England was between Bramley and Hambleton in 1745. The first county match was in 1931 between Durham and a combined Lancashire and Cheshire side.

RIGHT: **OLD TRAFFORD, 1910.** Lancashire Cricket Club team members pose for a photograph. This was a memorable season which saw some exciting matches with Lancashire finishing fourth in the League. By a remarkable coincidence, two sets of brothers (both by the name of Tyldesley) played first-class cricket for the county in this year.

LEFT: **OLD TRAFFORD, MAY 4 1938.** Warwick Road has been the home of Lancashire County Cricket Club since 1856 and international matches have been played there since 1884. In this, the first match of the season, two players walk out to the crease in a match between Lancashire and Worcestershire. Lancashire won by 10 wickets.

ABOVE: **ROCHDALE HORNETS, 1950.** Formed in 1871, Rochdale Hornets were founder members of the Rugby League. The club were at their strongest in the first two decades of the 20th century and won the Challenge Cup in the 1921-22 season. For most of their history until 1988, Hornets played at the famous Rochdale Athletics Ground.

ABOVE: **ROCHDALE HORNETS GRANDSTAND CRASH, 1939.** Tragedy struck at the Athletics Ground on April 1 when the main stand collapsed. Two spectators were killed and 15 others taken to hospital. The ground was packed when the roof of the stand gave way under the weight of spectators climbing onto the roof to get a better view.

THE CITY AT WAR

Manchester played a major role in both world wars and supplied large numbers of troops and armaments. As a centre of heavy industry, the city suffered badly from bombing during the Second World War. In true tradition, Manchester people rallied round to protect the vulnerable and to help defeat the enemy

ABOVE: **ALBERT SQUARE, 1915.** Lord Kitchener visits Manchester. Kitchener had completely re-organised the army into 69 divisions by April 1915, 30 of which were made up of volunteers, many from Manchester and Liverpool.

ABOVE: **USA TANK BOYS, SALFORD DOCKS, 1914.** Although American force did not enter the First World War until April 1917, the US regularly sent boats with equipment and specialist help to the Allies throughout the early years of the war.

ABOVE: **COLLYHURST, 1940.** In true *Dad's Army* fashion, a proud Home Guard battalion marches through Collyhurst. These volunteers had been promised uniforms and arms but as can be seen here their uniform consisted of little more than a roughly made arm band and their weapons amounted to a collection of pitchforks, broomsticks and makeshift rifles.

LEFT: **EVACUATION, 1939.** During September 1939, 72,000 children and 32,000 adults were voluntarily evacuated from the city. Some went as far afield as the Lake District but many only moved to the edge of the city to avoid the worst of the bombing. Towards the end of the war, when bombing was at its most intense in the south of the country, many children were moved from London to Manchester.

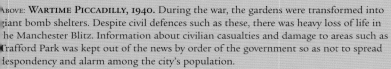

ABOVE: **WARTIME PICCADILLY, 1940.** During the war, the gardens were transformed into giant bomb shelters. Despite civil defences such as these, there was heavy loss of life in the Manchester Blitz. Information about civilian casualties and damage to areas such as Trafford Park was kept out of the news by order of the government so as not to spread despondency and alarm among the city's population.

THE MANCHESTER BLITZ, TOP, ABOVE AND LEFT. Between July 1940 and June 1941, Manchester suffered a number of devastating air raids. The raids on the nights of December 22 and 23 were particularly bad killing over 700 people and badly damaging Manchester Cathedral, Old Trafford football ground and the Royal Exchange. The Free Trade Hall (top) was left in ruins. Manchester had been hit by one of the heaviest incendiary attacks of the war and a firestorm quickly engulfed much of the city centre. Spectators reported seeing the flames from the moors 20 miles away. Winston Churchill (above) visits the devastated scene at the Free Trade Hall and St Peter's Street after the December raids. The prime minister surveys the ruins as he stands with local dignitaries amidst the carnage. The Free Trade Hall was so extensively damaged that it was not re-opened until 1951.

IN AND AROUND MANCHESTER

Originally a collection of separate towns and villages, the many districts around the city gradually merged into one urban area. Each district retained its own distinctive character: the areas to the north of the centre reflect much of the city's industrial past, while the leafy southern side, which was originally home to the wealthy cotton barons and industrialists, soon became the fashionable place to live for Manchester's middle-class professionals

RIGHT: **SALFORD CENTRAL LIBRARY AND ART GALLERY, 1958.** The *Then and Now* exhibition is in full swing as beautifully dressed girls in 1950s frocks make their way towards the entrance. Built in the 1850s the gallery forms the centrepiece of a set of buildings. It houses a fine collection of Victorian art and sculpture; the paintings of LS Lowry were displayed in the gallery before Salford's new Lowry centre was built.

LEFT AND BELOW: **DRINKING FOUNTAIN, 1890 & CHEETHAM HILL VILLAGE, 1905.** In Victorian times Cheetham was one of Manchester's most desirable areas. The historic home of Manchester's Jewish community, it boasts some of the city's most important institutions including Chetham's School. In recent decades it has become somewhat rundown but is now the focus of a major regeneration programme which will see the transformation of the area.

ABOVE: **ANCOATS, 1900.** Civic dignitaries at the laying of a foundation stone at the Pipe Stores off Oldham Road. Just a short walk from the city centre, Ancoats was the world's first industrial suburb. In the mid 19th century it was packed with back-to-back houses for the workers who laboured in the area's textile mills. Many of the surviving mills are now listed and Ancoats today is a conservation area.

RIGHT, BELOW AND FAR RIGHT: **THREE VIEWS OF CRUMPSALL.** The first, an aerial view from 1925 is of Crumpsall, Manchester and Prestwich Hospital; the British Dyestuffs Corporation and Crumpsall Vale are in the background. The hospital was built between 1866-70 and was designed by the architect Thomas Worthington (1826-1909). Originally the Prestwich Union workhouse, the buildings are now part of the North Manchester General Hospital. The second, a postcard from 1924, is of the Church of St Matthew with St Mary, Cleveland Road. The third dates from 1907 and shows pupils and staff at Crumpsall Lane Municipal School.

ST. MATTHEW'S CHURCH, CRUMPSALL.

LEFT: **HARPURHEY, 1934.** Postmen pass the time of day at the junction of Rochdale Road and Queens Road. Like neighbouring Crumpsall, Moston and Blackley, Harpurhey became a centre for dyeing and bleaching. Andrews Dyeworks came to dominate the town's commercial affairs. Harpurhey Cemetery, later to become the Manchester General Cemetery, was opened in 1868 with landscaped gardens and a catacomb. The country village of Harpurhey was soon swallowed up by industrialisation in the late 19th century and was incorporated into Manchester in 1885.

LEFT AND ABOVE: **TWO VIEWS OF BLACKLEY: CRAB LANE 1908 AND BOOTH HALL CHILDREN'S HOSPITAL** *c* **1959.** The Booth Hall Infirmary was built in 1907 using the rubble from the house of local philanthropist Humphrey Booth. In 1914 the hospital developed a children's unit which rapidly became one of the leading children's hospitals in the country.

LEFT: **MOSTON BOTTOMS, 1934.** The Irk Valley region was a flourishing mining community and contained many properties like these small cottages in the Bottoms. This was the original home of the Moston Brook animal sanctuary, an 'informal' sanctuary that was a feature of the locality in the 1950s.

RIGHT: **COLLYHURST, 1909.** A cottage in Hendham Vale, part of the Irk Valley, which was demolished in 1917. The Queen's Road railway viaduct is in the distance. Collyhurst had once been a leafy suburb but the discovery of coal in the mid 19th century led to its rapid expansion with many houses being built for the workers at St George's Colliery. By the end of the century Collyhurst was heavily industrialised and very polluted with a dye works, papermill, rope works and brickworks all belching fumes into the atmosphere.

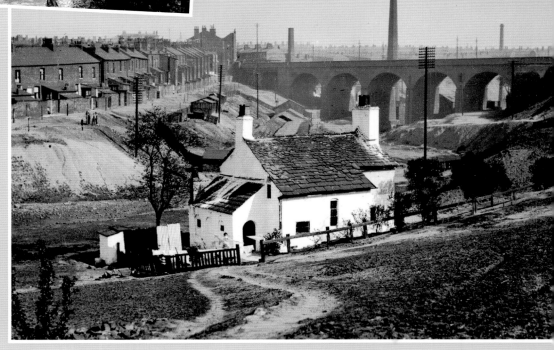

RIGHT: **CLAYTON, 1928.** A tram glides along the cobbled surface of Ashton New Road as people cross near the handsome Conservative Club. The Industrial Revolution propelled Clayton from its earlier status as a small village into a hive of industry. Its position close to the Ashton Canal meant that it was an important link in the transport network but it was also the site of a chemical works, which led to pollution in the nearby River Medlock. While decline and dereliction followed after the war, Clayton is now benefiting from the influx of funds associated with the development of the City of Manchester Stadium (the site of the 2002 Commonwealth Games).

RIGHT: **MILES PLATTING,** *c* **1936.** A view of the Oldham Road and Queens Road area. For much of the 19th and early 20th centuries Miles Platting was an area of densely-packed workers' housing, textile mills, a tannery, gasworks and a chemical works carved through by railway lines and sidings. Buildings were covered in soot and grime and the area was heavily polluted.

ABOVE AND LEFT: views of **BESWICK** and neighbouring **OPENSHAW** that could have come straight from *Coronation Street*. Both taken in 1963, the children above are in the doorway of the Rowsley Arms on the corner of Edenson Street while those on the left are standing on the corner of Bowness Street.

In post-war years the streetscape of Beswick and Openshaw changed fundamentally as the Victorian terraces were swept away in slum clearance programmes.

For most of the last two centuries heavy industry dominated the area with two massive concerns located nearby — the Armstrong Whitworth Ordnance Factory and the Beyer Peacock locomotive yards. These two enterprises sucked in workers and the population expanded dramatically in the 19th century. The decline of heavy industry in the 20th century saw the population fall to a fraction of its previous figure; now the people of Openshaw and Beswick are benefiting from regeneration and looking forward to the arrival of new businesses in the area.

LEFT AND BELOW: **TWO VIEW** **OF ARDWICK.** The busy Stockport Road, seen below in 1934, runs through Ardwick into th city centre. By the late 19th century the pleasant suburb had been absorbe into the grimy heart of Manchester and had its share of mills and other kinds of "works" along the River Medlock. Between 1879-1880 a school for the education of poor boys was built or Hyde Road, Ardwick. Called the Nicholls Hospital, its architect wa Thomas Worthington — the runner-up in the competition to build Manchester Town Hall. I was financed from a bequest by Benjamin Nicholls, the son of a local mill-owning family who died at the age o 36. During the Second World War it was used as a barracks for troops, the pupils having been transferred to Chethams School. In 1953 it was purchased by the local education authority and re-opened as the Nicholl County Secondary School for Boys. In 2002 the buildin was magnificently restored and is now the Manchester College for Arts and Technology.

LEFT: **STOCKPORT ROAD, LONGSIGHT 1958.** Longsight's earliest development owes much to its position on the ancient road between Buxton and Manchester. At the junction of Slade Lane and the Stockport Road there w a toll booth around which other buildings soon gather In the 1830s, the establishment and expansion of Belle Gardens fuelled development which was also helped by location of railway maintenance yards in the area.

ABOVE: **IN SEARCH OF A STORY.** By 1960, the Longsight Free Christian church in Birch Lane was being used by the BBC.

ABOVE: **SUNNYBROW PARK, GORTON,** c 1906. Adults and children enjoy the pleasures of Sunnybrow Park. In the distance is Brookfield Unitarian Church. It was built in 1870 and endowed by Richard Peacock, an engineer who became Gorton's first MP.

ABOVE: **TAN YARD BROW, GORTON,** 1904. A tannery operated in this area until 1958 giving this hill its distinctive name. The green spaces of Debdale Park off the Hyde Road provided locals with welcome relief from the bustle of the local streets and factories.

ABOVE: a rush cart outside the **PLOUGH HOTEL, GORTON,** c 1910. In the week before the annual rush-bearing ceremony in the local churches, a cart was taken round each of the local hotels and pubs in turn. On the day itself, fresh rushes were laid in each church and the old rushes burnt along with the cart.

ABOVE: LEAF STREET BATHS, HULME, 1920.
This splendid establishment was built in 1860 by the architect Thomas Worthington. Along with Turkish baths and more conventional "single" baths, Leaf Street also boasted a laundry and state of the art spin-dryers. These facilities were vitally important for the residents of Hulme: the once leafy village saw its population grow from 1,677 in 1801 to more than 150,000 by the mid 19th century. Most people lived in appalling conditions — one contemporary report speaks of up to 300 people sharing one lavatory.

BELOW: GROCER'S SHOP HULME, 1939. In the days before superstores corner shops like this one flourished, providing everything from cooked meat and cheese, to yeast, snuff and household goods.

LEFT: TRAFFORD PARK, *c* 1910.
By the early years of the 20th century the Ship Canal was helping to bring new prosperity to Manchester. Within 10 years of its opening more than 40 companies had moved to the newly established Trafford Park industrial estate, establishing this as the world's first industrial park. By 1945 over 75,000 people worked there. The triumphal arch, pictured here, was erected for a trade exhibition.

RIGHT: **LEVENSHULME, 1907.** Levenshulme is situated on the Manchester to Stockport Road. In the centre of the picture is the Levenshulme Town Hall. The council offices were moved in 1950 when the town was incorporated into the city of Manchester; the town hall is now the Levenshulme Antiques Village. The two sets of tramlines carried passengers from Manchester to Bullock Smithy.

LEFT: **WILMSLOW ROAD, FALLOWFIELD,** *c* 1910. A tram on its way into the city centre passes elegantly dressed ladies seated on Wilmslow Road. This tram called at Lapwing Lane terminus before reaching Rusholme.

ABOVE: **FIRE STATION, MOSS SIDE, 1906.** The Moss Side Fire Brigade proudly display their fire engine outside the new fire station. Built in the Alexandra Park area, the fire station and equipment was an example of the facilities that new wealth was bringing to the city.

LEFT: **NEW SCHOOL, MOSS SIDE, 1893.** Crowds gather around the site of the Princess Road Board School to watch the ceremony of the laying of the foundation stone. The size of the gathering shows the importance of the occasion for the local community.

Above: **CHORLTON GREEN, 1928.** Even today, Chorlton-cum-Hardy retains the feel of a country village. A group gather in front of the Horse and Jockey public house overlooking the picturesque Green. Although the original building dates from 1550 the pub only acquired its half-timbered façade around 1910.

Top right: **ZETLAND ROAD, CHORLTON, 1959.** The corner of Zetland Road, Sandy Lane and Barlow Moor Road appears an almost idyllic backwater with few vehicles in this late fifties photograph. The handsome Zetland Terrace built in 1883 dominates the view.

Right: **HORSE-DRAWN DELIVERY VAN, CHORLTON, 1949.** A Manchester and District Co-op bakery horse van stands on St Clements Road.

Above: **WITHINGTON, c 1910.** A view towards Withington village from the junction of Parsonage Road. The library is in the distance.

Above Right: **WITHINGTON, c 1950.** The same view 40 years later, this time looking down the road from the library, shows an increase in private cars and an absence of tramlines.

Left: **BURNAGE, c 1910.** Burnage was once described by George Bernard Shaw as the prettiest village in Manchester. The area developed a cottage industry in handweaving and many of the original weaver's cottages still exist in Burnage Lane. In 1910, Burnage Garden Village — a garden suburb — was built with many new semi-detached houses and recreational facilities including a village hall, allotments, tennis courts and a children's playground. The garden village was completed in 1912 and soon became a fashionable suburb for professional people and their families.

LEFT: **DIDSBURY, c 1935.** The Didsbury Hotel and Ye Olde Cock Inn built in 1909 stand either side of the entrance to Fletcher Moss House and Gardens, home of the former Alderman Fletcher Moss. The gateway was bought for £10 when the Spread Eagle Hotel was demolished.

BELOW: **GALLEON POOL, DIDSBURY, 1953.** Adults and children enjoy the outdoor Galleon Pool in Didsbury, not far from Parrs Wood junction. The area has now been developed as an hotel and leisure club.

ABOVE: **PUBLIC GARDENS DIDSBURY, 1957.** Fletcher Moss Gardens were given to the city in 1914 by Alderman Fletcher Moss, a keen botanist, who lived in the nearby parsonage. The -acre park and gardens became famous for their botanical -splays, orchid house and exotic plants.

LEFT: **RUSHOLME, c 1922.** This photograph is taken standing on Wilmslow Road, looking towards Dickenson Road with Platt Fields in the distance. The Birch Vale Hotel on the left-hand side attracted many local customers. It was in the Congregational church built on Wilmslow Road in 1864 that Herbert Asquith, later to become prime minister, married Helen Melland in 1867.

LEFT: **WYTHENSHAWE HALL,** *c* **1920.** This Tudor half-timbered house was the home of the Tatton family for over 400 years. Built around 1540, the family sold most of the surrounding land for housing development to Manchester City Council in 1926. The hall is still open for visitors today.

BELOW LEFT: **FISHMONGERS, NORTHENDEN, 1959.** On the corner of Brett Street, formerly Brown Street on Palatine Road, stands the famous seafood shop Mac Fisheries. Many older residents remember the tiled floors and marble counters.

BELOW: **CINEMA, NORTHENDEN, 1959.** The ABC or Forum Cinema opened in 1934. It contained a Wurlitzer organ and put on many stage shows. This Art Deco building has found a new use today as a meeting place for Jehovah's Witnesses.

Acknowledgment

Thanks to Sara, my eldest daughter, for all her help and support with the book.

Dedication

I have always had support and love from my mum and dad. I could not have done all that I have to date without their help. You will be with me always now and forever.

First published in 2009 by Myriad Books Limited
35 Bishopsthorpe Road London SE26 4PA

Photographs © Manchester City Library Archives and Local Studies Unit

Text © Robert Gibb
www.gibbsbookshop.co.uk

ISBN 1 84746 270 7 / 978 184746 270 1

Designed by Jerry Goldie Graphic Design

Printed in China

www.myriadbooks.com